Skateparks:

Grab Your Skateboard

By Matt Doeden

Content Consultant:
Pete Connelly
Staff writer, *Heckler* magazine

CAPSTONE
HIGH-INTEREST
BOOKS

an imprint of Capstone Press
Mankato, Minnesota

Capstone High-Interest Books are published by Capstone Press
151 Good Counsel Drive, P.O. Box 669, Mankato, Minnesota 56002
http://www.capstone-press.com

Library of Congress Cataloging-in-Publication Data
Doeden, Matt.
    Skateparks: grab your skateboard/by Matt Doeden.
    p. cm.—(Skateboarding)
    Includes bibliographical references and index.
    Summary: Describes the history of skateboarding parks, discussing some of
the top parks through the years.
    ISBN 0-7368-1072-2
    1. Skateboarding parks—United States—History—Juvenile literature.
2. Skateboarding parks—United States—Juvenile literature. [1. Skateboarding
parks—History. 2. Skateboarding—History.] I. Title. II. Series.
GV859.8 .D64 2002
796.22—dc21
                                                                    2001003921

Editorial Credits
Angela Kaelberer, editor; Timothy Halldin, cover designer, interior layout
    designer, and interior illustrator; Katy Kudela, photo researcher

Photo Credits
Capstone Press/Gary Sundermeyer, cover, 4, 7, 8, 12, 14, 16–17, 24, 26;
    Jim Foell, 29
SK8parkLIST.com, 11, 18, 20, 23

**Capstone Press thanks Adam Dagsgard and the skaters of Burnsville
Skate Park of Burnsville, Minnesota, and the staff and skaters of John
Rose OVAL in Roseville, Minnesota, for their assistance with this book.**

Table of Contents

Skateparks are safe places for skaters to practice.

About Skateparks

A skateboarder stands on the top of a ramp. The skater steps down hard on the skateboard. He speeds down the ramp and enters a huge skatepark.

The skater speeds toward a curved wooden ramp. He rides up to the top of the ramp. He jumps into the air and grabs the front end of the board. The skater then lands on the ramp and gets ready to try the trick again.

Learn About

- Pool skaters
- World's first skatepark
- Indoor and outdoor parks

Early Skateboard Parks

Skateparks were first built in the 1970s. Skaters were having a hard time finding places to practice their sport. Skateparks gave skaters safe places to skate.

Skaters in southern California started skating in empty backyard pools in the mid-1970s. But these pools were on private property. Property owners did not like the skaters using their pools. Parents, skate companies, and cities then got together to build safe places for the skaters to practice.

The world's first skateboarding park opened in Port Orange, Florida, in 1976. It was called Skateboard City. Another park opened one week later in Carlsbad, California. This park was called Carlsbad Park.

Most skateparks are outdoors.

Skateparks quickly became popular with skaters. Soon, people built skateparks in many North American cities. Skateparks also became popular in Australia, Europe, and Japan.

Most skateparks are outdoors. But indoor parks are common in areas that have cold temperatures. Some parks include both indoor and outdoor skating areas.

Skateparks include obstacles such as benches.

Elements

Each skatepark is different. But all parks share some common elements. These elements include obstacles such as bowls, ramps, stairs, and pyramids. Skaters perform tricks on each of these obstacles. Skilled skaters can perform tricks using several obstacles.

Flow is important to a skatepark. A skatepark's flow results from the placement of its obstacles. A park with good flow allows skaters to keep their speed while performing tricks.

Learn About

- Concrete obstacles
- Ramps
- Street obstacles

Concrete Obstacles

Most skateparks include bowls. Bowls look like empty swimming pools. They are made of smooth concrete and have transition. This area is the part of the bowl that curves from the flat bottom to the vertical walls.

Bowls also have a raised concrete area around the top of the vertical wall. This area is called coping. Skaters perform grinds by sliding their skateboards' trucks across the coping. They perform slides by sliding their wheels across the coping.

Full pipes are concrete tubes. Many early skateparks had full pipes. Newer parks did not include these obstacles. But today, full pipes are again popular with skaters. Several cities have built full pipes into their skateparks. These cities include Calgary in Canada and Quito in Ecuador.

Bowls have a raised area called coping.

A snake run is a series of rounded corners and sloped areas called banks. It looks like a snake built into the concrete. Skaters ride from bank to bank through the snake run. They try to keep their speed up for the ride back.

Snake runs have hips. Hips look like the curves in the letter "S." Skaters use these areas to jump across the snake run. They often perform tricks as they jump.

Half-pipes are shaped like the letter "U."

Ramps

Skatepark structures built from wood are called ramps. Ramps are among the most popular skatepark features.

Half-pipe ramps are shaped like the letter "U." Skaters call these ramps half-pipes because they look like half of a full pipe. Half-pipes also are known as vert ramps. They usually are between 8 and 12 feet (2.4 and 3.7 meters) high.

Modern half-pipes are wide. Like bowls, they have vertical walls and transition. They have more flat surface on the bottom than a full pipe does. Half-pipes also have steel coping at the top of the transitions. Skaters ride back and forth to try to reach the coping. Many skaters do tricks above the coping. These tricks are called aerials or airs.

Many parks also have mini-ramps. Mini-ramps usually are between 3 and 6 feet (.9 and 1.8 meters) high. Many skateparks place several mini-ramps of different sizes in one area to form a course. This course looks much like a snake run.

Skaters perform tricks on railings.

In 2001, the International Association of Skateboard Companies said that more than 300 skateparks existed or were being built in the United States. New skateparks open every day in cities throughout North America.

Street Obstacles and Pyramids

Many skatepark obstacles are designed to look like obstacles found on a street or sidewalk. These obstacles include stairs, hand railings, and ledges. Skaters perform slides and grinds on these obstacles.

Many skateparks have pyramids. Most of these wooden or concrete boxes have four sloped sides that meet to form a flat surface at the top. Skaters do ollies or other tricks on pyramids.

Bank ramp

Jump ramp

Quarterpipe

Rollover

Bench

Ledge

Railing

17

Curt Pernice Skate Park is a popular California park.

Best of the Best

Skateparks first became popular in California. Today, California is home to some of the most famous parks in the world.

Many skaters say that Curt Pernice Skate Park is the best public skatepark in California. This park opened in February 2001 in Ripon, California. The park covers about 25,000 square feet (2,300 square meters). The park has many vertical walls and long snake runs. Skaters say the park has excellent flow.

Learn About

- Curt Pernice Skate Park
- Vans Skate Park
- Oregon skateparks

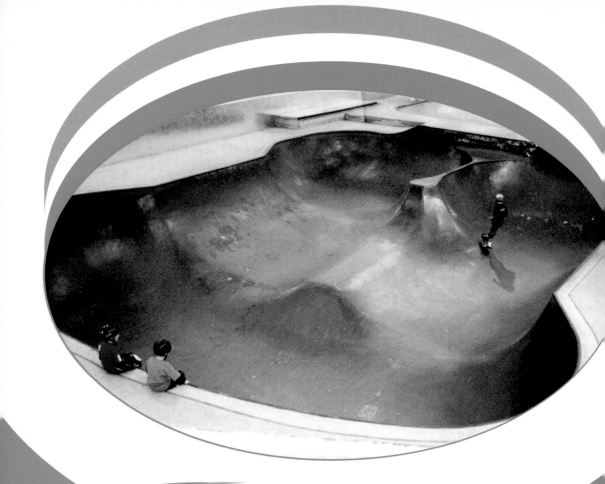

Vans Skate Park is one of the world's largest skateparks.

Only one of the skateparks built in the United States in the 1970s still exists today. This park is Kona Skatepark in Jacksonville, Florida. Some 1970s skateparks still exist in places such as Spain, Brazil, and Australia.

Vans Skate Park

In 1998, Vans Shoe Company built the Vans Skate Park in Orange, California. The park is one of the largest in the world. It covers 46,000 square feet (4,273 square meters) of land. All but 6,000 square feet (557 square meters) of the park is indoors. Part of the skatepark is reserved for beginning skaters.

Vans Skate Park has ramps of different sizes. One of these ramps is 80 feet (24 meters) wide.

The park also has a street course and a round bowl connected to a square pool. This bowl is 12 meters (3.7 feet) deep. It is a copy of the famous Combi Bowl at Upland Skatepark in Upland, California. That park was built in 1977 and torn down in 1989.

Oregon Parks

Oregon also is home to many top skateparks. Burnside Skatepark is one of the most famous parks in the world. Skaters started building this park in 1990 under the Burnside Bridge in Portland, Oregon. They continued adding to the park during the next 10 years.

Burnside has been included in several skateboarding videos and video games. These videos include *Scorchin' Summer, The Mission,* and *Fruit of the Vine.*

Medford Skate Park in Medford also is located in Oregon. It opened in May 2000. Medford has a bowl that is 10 feet (3 meters) deep. This bowl has concrete coping. The park also has a snake run with hips that work well for ollies.

Newberg Skatepark opened July 1, 2000, in Newberg, Oregon. The skaters who built Burnside also built Newberg. The skaters' company is called Dreamland Designs.

The bowl at Medford Skate Park is 10 feet (3 meters) deep.

The park's 29,000 square feet (2,700 square meters) of concrete includes half-pipes, bowls, and a BMX track. It also has a curved railing called the Dragon Rail and a six-sided volcano pyramid. The volcano is topped with a spinning concrete wheel. Skaters stall their boards on top of the spinning wheel and skate down in another direction.

Safe skaters always wear helmets.

CHAPTER FOUR

Enjoying Skateparks

Skaters can help keep skateparks safe. They should wear helmets to protect their head. Skaters also should wear elbow and knee pads.

Skaters should skate within their limits. Beginning skaters should start by skating on mini-ramps. Skaters who feel confident about skating on mini-ramps can move up to half-pipes and street obstacles.

Skaters who are seriously hurt may need medical attention. Nearby skaters should immediately ask park officials for help. Park officials may call a doctor or an ambulance.

Learn About

- Skatepark safety
- Rules and waivers
- Building a skatepark

Park Rules

Skaters must follow the rules of each park. Most parks post their rules in a noticeable place. Skaters should read the rules before they begin skating. Skaters who break the rules may be forced to leave the park.

Many parks require skaters to sign waivers. These legal documents say that the park's management is not responsible for injuries. Skaters use these parks at their own risk.

Skaters also must respect other skaters. Parks often are crowded. Skaters can avoid crashes by staying out of one another's way. Respecting others allows all skaters to use the park safely.

Many skateparks have grind boxes.

Building a Skatepark in Your City

Skaters need a place to practice. Skateparks allow skaters to practice in an environment that is safe and fun. Skaters who want a skatepark in their city can follow these steps:

1.   Organize a group of skaters and parents.

2.   Collect signatures from people in town who support building a skatepark.

3.   Go to a city council meeting and show city officials the need for a skatepark.

4.   Work with city officials to help plan the skatepark. The planning stage is very important. Skaters should help with the planning from the beginning of construction to the opening day. The city will have a better park if everyone works together.

Words to Know

aerial (AIR-ee-uhl)—a stunt or trick performed in the air

concrete (KON-kreet)—a building material made from a mixture of sand, gravel, cement, and water; many skateparks are made of concrete.

obstacle (OB-stuh-kuhl)—an object such as a ramp or a railing; skaters perform tricks on obstacles.

pyramid (PIHR-uh-mid)—a sloped skateboarding obstacle; most skatepark pyramids include four sides that meet to form a flat surface at the top.

waiver (WAY-vuhr)—a legal document that protects skatepark owners from injury lawsuits

To Learn More

Burke, L. M. *Skateboarding! Surf the Pavement.* The Extreme Sports Collection. New York: Rosen Publishing, 1999.

Freimuth, Jeri. *Extreme Skateboarding Moves.* Behind the Moves. Mankato, Minn.: Capstone High-Interest Books, 2001.

Hoena, B. A. *Skateboards: Designs and Equipment.* Skateboarding. Mankato, Minn.: Capstone High-Interest Books, 2002.

Useful Addresses

Skatepark Association of the United States of America
2118 Wilshire Boulevard, Suite 622
Santa Monica, CA 90403

Transworld Skateboarding Magazine
353 Airport Road
Oceanside, CA 92054

Internet Sites

Skatepark Association of the United States of America
http://www.spausa.org

Skatepark.org
http://skatepark.org

Suburban Rails
http://www.suburbanrails.com/pages/plguide.html

Index